Real Money Matters:
A Complete Handbook for
Millennial Financial Success

ANAS AMINU

DEDICATION

I dedicate this work to my beloved father, my mother and the entire family and friends for their guidance, constant prayers and timeless support both morally and financially towards attaining success.

Contents

INTRODUCTION

Financial literacy is having the necessary knowledge to make good decisions about your money. The importance of being financially literate ties directly to one's chances of growing and managing wealth.

To effectively manage and increase one's money, a person must fully understand five essential talents. As follows:

1. Income

The capacity to earn is the first pillar of wealth building. Always look for ways to make money. Simply said, earning is the act of bringing money home from a job, self-employment, or various investments.

You must make a plan on how to maximize your revenue as soon as you start earning it. The amount you plan to save, invest, and spend must then be taken into account. The process of managing and increasing wealth begins here.

2. Investments and Savings

Simply said, saving is the practice of laying money aside for future emergencies or other costs. Contrarily, investing is the process of purchasing securities such as bonds, stocks, and real estate with the intention of increasing your financial returns.

Earning money alone won't allow you to increase your wealth; in fact, most people consider saving money and investing it to be the most crucial of all financial literacy skills. Your ability to manage and increase your wealth may depend on how diligently you save and invest.

3. Spending

Spending is a crucial idea since it can be a representation of your values, way of life, and most significantly, your financial behavior. To be successful in the effort to restrict expenditure, every person needs to be able to distinguish between NEEDS and WANTS.

Spending restraint is a crucial component of properly managing your wealth. The most effective technique someone can use to restrict spending and establish a foundation for saving and investing is the capacity to develop a budget and adhere to it scrupulously.

4. Borrowing

Borrowing is simply the act of acquiring debts. Borrowing when needed isn't a bad move especially when a payment structure is provided to the payee. Acquiring debts such as business loans to create job opportunities or build businesses, and real estate investments, are good examples of how borrowed money can be turned into assets and wealth accumulation. The only time when borrowing can become a problem is when one borrows to satisfy a want, which should be avoided as much as possible if one wants to accumulate wealth.

5. Protecting

Protecting in terms of financial literacy refers to all the plans to protect everything you have acquired, yourself and, your loved ones. Protecting everything you love and have worked for, requires that one partner with a trustworthy brand.

BENEFITS OF FINANCIAL LITERACY

- Ability to differentiate between wants and needs.

- It helps to create a good savings culture.

- Increases your chances of creating a secure financial future.

- Helps you manage your wealth better.

- Helps you manage your debts better.

- Financial literacy helps you with budget creation.

THE FINANCIAL CHALLENGES FACED BY MILLENNIALS

Millennials, those born between 1981 and 1996, deal with particular financial difficulties. Many of you are struggling with high housing costs, a shifting employment environment, and significant student loan debt. Feeling overburdened or concerned about your financial future is not unusual.

But facing these obstacles head-on is the first step towards overcoming them. You can use these difficulties as chances for growth and financial stability by developing a proactive financial mindset.

THE CONSEQUENCES OF FINANCIAL IGNORANCE

Let's think about the effects of financial illiteracy to emphasize how crucial financial literacy is. You can become stuck in a debt cycle, unable to save for your aspirations, or unclear about your financial future if you lack a good financial education.

THE POWER OF GOAL SETTING

Financial success is not a coincidence. A vision and a plan come first. Setting specific financial objectives gives your money direction and a purpose. Goals help you get there, whether you desire to buy a house, tour the world, retire well, or simply create a safety net.

FINANCIAL MANAGEMENT

Financial Management is that part of management which is concerned mainly with raising funds in the most economic and suitable manner; using these funds as profitably (for a given risk level) as possible; planning future operations, and controlling current performance and future developments through financial accounting, budgeting, statistical analysis and other means (Ogunniyi, 2010; p. 1).

OBJECTIVES OF FINANCIAL MANAGEMENT

The major objective of management is to maximize the shareholders' wealth. The shareholders' wealth is the present value of future cash flows or present value of future dividends payable to the shareholders infinitely. The Shareholders wealth maximization is gradually becoming the single and narrow objective of firms pursued by financial managers making it the most fashionable objective of the firm. This is being achieved through a combination of goals such as:

i.   Increase in the market share of the firm
ii.   ii. Increase in reported profits
iii.   iii. Continuous survival of the business
iv.   iv. Provision of valued services to customers
v.   v. Ensuring public acceptability of the firm and its products/services coupled with both social acceptability and legal acceptability.

FUNCTIONS OF THE FINANCIAL MANAGER/ROLES OF FINANCIAL MANAGEMENT

i.   Financial Decision: This is the effective management of the capital structure of the business. The financial manager must ensure maximum mixture of debt and equity in financing the firm, so as to ensure maximum returns to the shareholders

The maximum mix of finance of debt and equity must be established to maximize the returns of shareholders

ii. Investment Decision: This involves the identification of viable projects. The financial manager should select the most profitable investment portfolio that will reduce to the barest minimum the risk of the organization not maximizing stockholders' wealth.

iii. Acquisition Decision: The financial manager must be interested in the organizations internal and external growth. The growth of corporate organization can be varied, either by way of merger or acquisition, by backward integration or forward integration etc.

iv. Working Capital Management (Treasury Management): It is the totality of management of cash, debtor prepayments, stocks creditors, short term loans accruals, etc. to ensure the profitability of the firm's operation. It is the management of current asset and liabilities of firm, which is fast becoming important in the face of high cost of capital. In modern financial world, efficient management of the working capital will ensure maximum utilization of scarce financial resource and ipso facto maximization of the shareholder's wealth.

SOURCES OF FINANCE

There are different forms and sources of finance available to the firm. These are both internal and external; they may be used singularly or in combination. The term "source of business finance" is used to refer to the means by which an entrepreneur raises capital to establish and operate the business of his/her choice (Ogundele, 2012; p. 633).

SHORT TERM SOURCES OF FINANCE

Short term sources of finance are financing sources up to one-year duration (i.e. they are repayable within one year). It is suitable for funding shortages in working capital. They should not, if it can be avoided, be used to finance a long-term investment. A company that funds long term project with short term funds may be forced to renegotiate a long-term loan under unfavorable condition or to sell the asset,

11

which is needed for the continuation of the business. In addition, where short term sources are recalled by the holders, a company might find itself in a position of technical or legal bankruptcy. The main methods of obtaining short-term funds are:

i.   Borrowing from friends and relations
ii.   Borrowing from co-operatives
iii. Trade credits (Suppliers) involves buying of goods on credit. In other words, it is the purchase or sales of goods or equipment whose payment would be effective at a future date. It is a facility granted to a company by a supplier since the system allows the company to pay at a later date

MEDIUM TERM SOURCES OF FINANCE

These are financing sources between 1 to 5 years' duration. Some of the medium term sources of finance include:

i.   Medium Term loans: These are usually issued for a definite period when compared with overdraft. This is a negotiated loan between a financial institution and a company between 1-5 years, usually at a fixed rate of interest. Medium Term Loans in form of bank lending can be secured or unsecured. Unsecured lending is not common and is only available to credit worthy companies. Secured lending requires heavy collateral securities and proper evaluation of credit worthiness of all customers are also considered.

ii.   Hire purchase agreement: This is in form of a credit sales agreement by which the owner of the assets or supplier grant the purchaser the right to take possession of the assets but ownership will not pass until all the hire purchase payment has been paid. The purchaser will pay the hire purchase payment over an agreed period. No form of collateral is required. It is normally reflected in the balance sheet of the borrower. It reduces the gearing ratio and increases ability to raise further finance. It also attracts capital allowance.

iii. Lease: A lease is a contractual agreement between the owner of an asset (lessor) and the user of the asset (lessee) granting the user or lessee the exclusive right to use the asset for an agreed period in return for the payment of rent. The main advantage of lending to a lessee is the use of an asset without having to buy.

iv. Sales and leaseback: This is an arrangement by which a firm sells its assets to a financial institution for cash and the financial institution immediately leases it back to the firm.

v. Venture capital: This is a major source of capital for SMEs and collapsed businesses. The provider of finance might decide to participate in the company instead of allowing the client to run the business himself. The participation might be in the form of equity or debenture stock.

LONG TERM SOURCES

These are financing sources of 5 years and more duration. Long term sources of finance include:

i) Loan Stock/Debentures: This is long-term debt

finance raised by a company for which interest is paid usually at a fixed rate. The company must pay the interest whether it makes profit or not. Loan stock also has a nominal value of ₦100. Debentures are a form of loan stock that is legally defined as the written acknowledgement of a debt incurred by a company usually given under company seal and containing provisions as to the payment of interest and eventual repayment of principal.

ii)   Preference Shares: The holders of preference shares are entitled to a fixed percentage dividend before ordinary shareholders can be paid any dividend. Preference shares are a form of hybrid security between ordinary shares and debentures. These are often issued as an alternative to debt when the company pays no tax. Preference shares can be redeemable or irredeemable.

iii)   Ordinary Shares: Ordinary shareholders are the owners of the firm. They exercise control over the firm through their voting rights. A firm contemplating on raising funds through ordinary shares will incur floatation cost/issue cost.

BUDGETING BASICS

Budgeting is about empowerment, not constraint. It enables you to make deliberate decisions about your spending by helping you to understand where your money is going.

A budget is a tool that expresses activities in financial terms. It shows the money you need to spend to carry out your planned activities. The money you need to spend is called expenditures or costs. The money you need to make/receive is called income.

WHY IS A BUDGET IMPORTANT?

• A budget makes you think specifically about how much it will cost to pay for the activities you are planning versus how much money you actually have. The process of making a budget may make you realize that your plans are not realistic. This gives you a chance to rethink your activities and avoid financial problems in the future.

• A budget tells you when you will need certain amounts of money to carry out your activities.

• A budget lets you compare how much you think you will spend (projected costs) to how much you actually spent (actual costs).

• A budget promotes financial honesty, responsibility, and

transparency. A budget lets everyone see how much money has been received and spent, and compare this to the original plans. Then they can ask informed questions about differences between the two.

• You cannot raise money from donors without a budget.

Donors use budgets to decide if what you are asking for is reasonable and well planned.

CHARACTERISTICS OF A GOOD BUDGET

• Budgets cover a defined set of activities. This means that each individual project should have its own budget.

However, you should also combine all of the budgets into one overall operations budget—it is important to see the big picture.

• Budgets state the time period covered. You should make an annual budget and a budget that covers the whole life of a project. However, dividing the budget into months or quarters may make it easier to monitor.

• Budgets are realistic about expected income and expected costs. Managers often under- or overestimate costs. The financial problems that result from this can have a negative effect on program implementation, beneficiaries, and staff morale.

• Budgets include indirect costs. In addition to including direct costs (e.g., salaries, supplies), the budget must include indirect costs. These can include costs like pensions, insurance, and overhead (e.g., administration, services shared among various programs like internet, and telephones, rent).

• Budgets should be made in the donor's currency and then translated into local currency. This will make it easier to follow and implement.

• There should always be more than one person making and monitoring the budget to ensure accuracy, transparency, and accountability

HOW TO MAKE A BUDGET

1. Study your agreement with your donor carefully. Donors often have particular requirements about when money should be spent and what it should be spent on.

2. Review your plans. Review the activities you will do, when you will do them, and what resources you will need (human, financial, etc.). Program staff and financial staff should work on this process together. Your budget and your plans for activities must match exactly—everything you are planning must appear in your budget.

3. Gather the information you need and make sure it is up to date. You will need information about all kinds of income and expenditures (e.g., staff salaries, rent, donations, grants, past costs). You need to get information from all financial staff and project managers regarding their expenses.

4. Create your budget

• Follow donors' guidelines. Donors often require that you submit your budget in a specific format. If you do not do so, you could lose funding opportunities.

• Involve other staff members in the budgeting process (e.g., program, administration, finance staff).

• Present your budget clearly, so that it is easy for everyone to understand.

• Specify the dates covered by the budget.

• Include notes explaining budget items or calculations, when needed. For example, if certain funds have not yet been received, make a note.

• If you have access to a computer, making and monitoring your budget will be easier, but even without a computer, you can budget effectively. If you don't have a computer, you must pay extra attention to checking your calculations.

5. Check your math. Make sure that your figures are correct by having one or two other people review your calculations.

6. Compare your income to your expenditures. If they do not match, you need to rethink your plans.

7. When the budget is complete, share it with other staff. Orient them on what they have to do to follow the budget.

MONITORING YOUR BUDGET

Making your budget is the first step, and monitoring it is

the second. Keep a record of all your actual income and expenditures. Use documents like receipts, cash books, invoices, photocopies of checks, and staff timesheets to monitor your expenditures. Every expenditure must have a piece of documentation to support it.

Each month compare the records of what you are receiving and spending to your original budget and plan. This will help you see if you are spending more—or less—than you planned in any category. You need to avoid both over- and underspending. These comparisons will help you see if your project is on track from a spending perspective. If not, you need to know why. Then you have to determine if you need to slow down, speed up, or shift spending. You can do this for individual cost categories and for overall spending.

If you need to make changes to your budget, you must first consult your donors and explain the situation. Be sure to discuss all changes with other staff as well.

SAVING AND INVESTING
The Power of Investing:

As an investor, you have a lot of options for where to put your money. It's important to weigh types of investments carefully.

Investments are generally bucketed into three major categories: stocks, bonds and cash equivalents. There are many different types of investments within each bucket.

TYPES OF INVESTMENTS

Here are six types of investments you might consider for long-term growth, and what you should know about each

The types of investments are:

- Stocks
- Bonds
- Mutual funds
- Index funds
- Exchange-traded funds (ETFs)
- Options

Stocks:

A stock is an investment in a specific company. When you purchase a stock, you're buying a share — a small piece — of that company's earnings and assets. Companies sell shares of stock in their businesses to raise cash; investors can then buy and sell those shares among themselves. Stocks sometimes earn high returns but also come with more risk than other investments

Bonds:

A bond is a loan you make to a company or government. When you purchase a bond, you're allowing the bond issuer to borrow your money and pay you back with interest.

Mutual funds:

If the idea of picking and choosing individual bonds and stocks isn't your bag, you're not alone. In fact, there's an investment designed just for people like you: the mutual fund.

Index funds:

An index fund is a type of mutual fund that passively tracks an index, rather than paying a manager to pick and choose investments. For example, an S&P 500 index fund will aim to mirror the performance of the S&P 500 by holding stock of the companies within that index.

Exchange-traded funds:

ETFs are a type of index fund: They track a benchmark index and aim to mirror that index's performance. Like index funds, they tend to be cheaper than mutual funds because they are not actively managed.

Options:

An option is a contract to buy or sell a stock at a set price, by a set date. Options offer flexibility, as the contract doesn't actually obligate you to buy or sell the stock. As the name implies, doing so is an option. Most options contracts are for 100 shares of a stock.

RISK TOLERANCE AND INVESTMENT GOALS

Risk tolerance refers to the amount of loss an investor is prepared to handle while making an investment decision.

Investors are usually classified into three main categories based on how much risk they can tolerate. They include aggressive, moderate, and conservative.

Knowing the risk tolerance level helps investors plan their entire portfolio and will drive how they invest.

TYPES OF RISK TOLERANCE

Investors are usually classified into three main categories based on how much risk they can tolerate. The categories are based on many factors, few of which have been discussed above. The three categories are:

1. Aggressive

Aggressive risk investors are well versed with the market and take huge risks. Such types of investors are used to seeing large upward and downward movements in their portfolio. Aggressive investors are known to be wealthy, experienced, and usually have a broad portfolio.

2. Moderate

Moderate risk investors are relatively less risk-tolerant when compared to aggressive risk investors. They take on some risk and usually set a percentage of losses they can handle. They balance their investments between risky and safe asset classes. With the moderate approach, they earn lesser than aggressive investors when the market does well but does not suffer huge losses when the market falls.

3. Conservative

Conservative investors take the least risk in the market. They do not indulge in risky investments at all and go for the options they feel are safest. They prioritize avoiding losses above making gains. The asset classes they invest in are limited to a few, such as FD and PPF, where their capital is protected.

INVESTMENT GOALS

Investment goals are set based on current and future financial circumstances and depend on income, age, and future outlook

- Goals can be set using the SMART framework
- Risk tolerance is not only defined by personal preference but also the risks required to achieve each objective

- Asset allocation is where you choose how much you will invest in which investments, based on your goals
- Short-term goals (3 – 12 months) focus on preserving capital and are only suited to certain types of investments, whereas medium to long-term goals focus on wealth generation

RETIREMENT PLANNING

Retirement planning involves determining retirement income goals and what's needed to achieve those goals. Retirement planning includes identifying income sources, sizing up expenses, implementing a savings program, and managing assets and risk. Future cash flows are estimated to gauge whether the retirement income goal is possible.

You can start at any time, but it works best if you factor it into your financial planning as early as possible. That's the best way to ensure a safe, secure—and fun—retirement. The fun part is why it makes sense to pay attention to the serious and perhaps boring part: planning how you'll get there.

STEPS TO RETIREMENT PLANNING

Regardless of where you are in life, there are several key steps that apply to almost everyone during their retirement planning. The following are some of the most common:

i)   Come up with a plan. This includes deciding when you want to start saving when you want to retire, and how much you'd like to save for your ultimate goal.

ii)   Decide how much you'll set aside each month. Using automatic deductions takes away the guesswork, keeps you on track, and takes away the temptation to stop or forget depositing money on your own.

iii)   Choose the right accounts for you. Take the chance to invest in a 401(k) or similar account if your employer offers that option. Remember, if the company offers an employer match and you don't sign up, you're just giving away free money. And don't forget to have an emergency fund, which can be easily liquidated if you need cash in a pinch.

iv)   Check on your investments from time to time and make periodic adjustments. It's always a good idea to make any changes whenever there's a change in your lifestyle and when you enter a different stage in your life.

WHY IS RETIREMENT PLANNING SO IMPORTANT?

Retirement planning allows you to sock away enough money to maintain the same lifestyle you currently have. After all, no one wants to work right up until the end. While you may work part-time or pick up the odd gig here or there, it probably won't be enough to sustain your current lifestyle. And Social Security benefits will only take you so far. That's why it's so important to have a viable plan that allows you to get the maximum amount of money

RENTING VS. OWNING: PROS AND CONS

Renting a Home:

The biggest myth about renting is that you're throwing away money every month. This is not true. After all, you need a place to live, and that always costs money in one way or another. While it's true that you aren't building equity with monthly rent payments, not all of the costs of homeownership always go toward building equity.

Owning a Home:

Homeownership brings both tangible and intangible benefits. Not only do you have your own home, but you can make decisions about the look and design of the space, and you also get a sense of stability and pride of ownership.

PROS OF RENTING A HOME

Limited responsibilities: You are not saddled with the responsibility of maintaining the house or paying for major repairs. This can save you money and time.

Lower upfront payment: Renting a house does not require you to put down a huge amount of money—well, these days, that is debatable with the level of inflation in the economy but it is still a lot cheaper than making a down payment for buying a house. This is good if you don't have so much savings.

Flexibility: If you are one who likes to experience what living in different places will feel like, then you are better off renting because it gives you the flexibility to move when you need a change of location.

Cons of Renting a House

Lack of equity: Renting does not build equity since the house does not belong to you. This means you won't benefit from potential property value appreciation. Whatever money you pay benefits the homeowner.

No control over rent: You are at the mercy of your landlord when it comes to the increment in your rent. They can decide to review your tenancy agreement and increase your rent when it's time for renewal.

Restrictions on customization: You can't remodel or redesign to your taste because the house doesn't belong to you. If the house is dated and isn't too aesthetically pleasing, there is only so much you can do even if you have the means to change it because you do not own it.

No tax benefits: When you rent, you do not enjoy tax benefits such as deducting mortgage interest or property taxes unlike when you own.
Pros of Owning a Home

Investment opportunity: Owning a home can be a good investment strategy as the value appreciates over time and help you build equity.

Control: You have the liberty to do whatever renovations or remodeling you deem fit. You want your kitchen and living room to look different from what they looked like last Christmas? You got it!

Tax benefits: Homeowners may be able to deduct mortgage interest and property taxes from their taxes, providing valuable tax benefits.

Stability and security: Owning a home takes away the anxiety of someday getting a quit notice because the property has been sold or put to another use.

Cons

Financial commitment: Owning a home comes with significant upfront costs, including a down payment, closing costs, and ongoing expenses like property taxes, insurance, and maintenance.

Less flexibility: Owning a home can limit your flexibility, as it is more challenging to relocate quickly. Often times you need to sell the house to be able to relocate.

Maintenance and repairs: As a homeowner, you are responsible for the maintenance and repair costs, which can be expensive and time-consuming.

Market fluctuations: Property values can fluctuate, and there is a risk of losing money if the value of your home decreases or if you are forced to sell during a downturn.

THE IMPORTANCE OF A REAL ESTATE AGENT

Real estate agents help people buy, sell, and rent homes, land, and other properties. There's no national real estate license, so agents must meet their state's licensing requirements.

While the requirements vary by state, all aspiring agents must take a pre-licensing course from an accredited real estate school, take (and pass) their state exam, activate their license, and join a real estate brokerage.

Benefits of working with a real estate agent:

1. Better Access to Homes

2. Negotiation

3. Paperwork, Paperwork, Paperwork

4. Save Money

5. Guidance and Support

6. Finding the Right Homes

7. Avoid Closing Issues

TAXES AND FINANCIAL EFFICIENCY

Taxes are mandatory contributions levied on individuals or corporations by a government entity—whether local, regional, or national. Tax revenues finance government activities, including public works and services such as roads and schools, or programs such as Social Security and Medicare

Tax efficiency, defined as the process of organizing an investment so that it receives the least possible taxation, is as important in general investment as it is in business. Business, commercial investments, and even private investment vehicles can experience tax efficiency through planning. Any time a person has caused a change which avoids a higher tax rate they are experiencing the benefits of a change in their **tax efficiency rating**.

THE BASICS OF TAX DEDUCTIONS

A tax deduction is **an amount that you can deduct from your taxable income to lower the amount of taxes that you owe**. You can choose the standard deduction—a single deduction of a fixed amount—or itemize deductions on Schedule A of your income tax return.

Tax deductions have long been near and dear to American taxpayers for many reasons, specifically those that involve family, homes, charities, and other things many taxpayers value. A tax deduction is a legal means to reduce a taxpayer's taxable income. Tax deductions are taken out of taxable income (also known as adjusted gross income), thus lowering a taxpayer's overall tax liability.

Tax deductions can result from a variety of transactions and other events over the course of the year. It's important for taxpayers to grasp how tax deductions work and how they may or may not apply to their tax filing.

Two major tax deductions: Standard and itemized

When reporting federal income taxes, individuals and households typically choose between standard or itemized deductions.

A standard deduction is a single deduction at a fixed amount and varies depending on your income, age, and filing status, among other factors, and it changes each year.

An itemized deduction is a tax deduction that you take for various expenses you incurred during the tax year. These deductions include a range of expenses that are only deductible when you choose to itemize.

INSURANCE AND RISK MANAGEMENT

Insurance is a means of protection from financial loss in which, in exchange for a fee, a party agrees to compensate another party in the event of a certain loss, damage, or injury. It is a form of risk management, primarily used to hedge against the risk of a contingent or uncertain loss.

Risk management is a broad topic. It involves taking steps to minimize the likelihood of things going wrong, a concept known as loss control. It also involves the purchasing of insurance to reduce the financial impact of adverse events on a company when, despite your best efforts, bad things happen. No one likes thinking about what could go wrong. Nevertheless, as a prudent manager, you should understand the risks your business faces. Until you identify risks, you can't make good decisions about managing them.

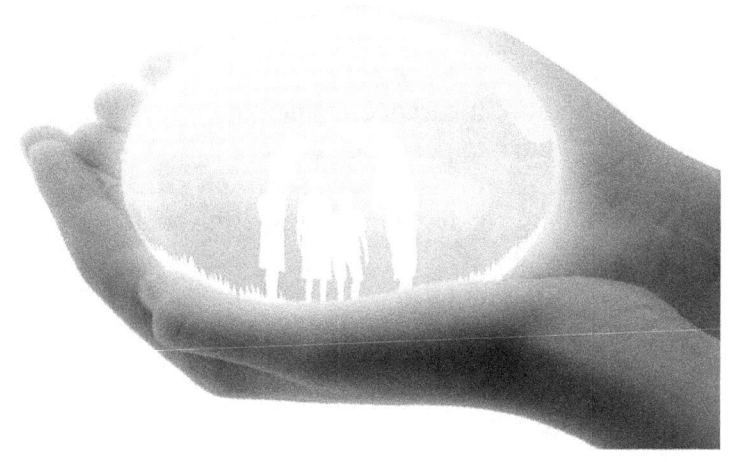

TYPES OF INSURANCE POLICIES

You can divide the insurance based on the type of coverage it is providing as below:

Life Insurance Policy:

> It is insurance on your life. You buy life insurance to ensure that your loved ones are financially secured even when you are not around. If you are the only breadwinner, you would want your family members to maintain the same living standards in the event of your untimely demise. The nominee gets the sum assured in case of your death.

Health Insurance Policy:

> Although health insurance is usually counted as a general insurance contract, there are a few differences. Health insurance covers your medical costs for

expensive treatments. You can avail two types of health insurance policies:

1. Mediclaim Insurance, which compensates you for the medical expenses
2. Critical Health Insurance, which offers lump-sum payments for dangerous and life-threatening health conditions

Non-life Insurance Policy:

These compensate for the losses sustained arising from a specific financial event that is not related to life. Non-life insurance could be car insurance, home insurance, etc.

You can avail insurance benefits under the following two types of policies:

Because of these two variants health insurance falls perfectly between general and life insurance policies. Also, both health insurance policies are important in ensuring complete financial safety for you and your family.

BENEFITS OF INSURANCE

There are a lot of benefits of buying insurance and listed below are some of them:

Financial Safety for Family:

They provide cover against life's uncertainties and protect you against losses arising from different unexpected events in life.

Safety of Financial Status:

Certain events like medical emergencies can have a significant impact on your cash flow management. Insurance ensures you don't have to pay out of pocket for such situations.

Wealth Creation Goals:

Insurance policies like ULIPs give you investment opportunities and help you fulfil your essential financial goals.

Wealth Preservation:

Life insurance policies like endowment and moneyback plans are some of the safest long-term investments possible. These plans help you preserve your wealth from inflation and taxes for long periods.

Wealth Distribution:

Few investment plans offer the kind of safety offered by life insurance pension plans. After retiring at the age of 60, you can live up to 100. Only life insurance pension plans can guarantee a regular income for that period.

FINANCIAL MILESTONES

Financial milestones are specific goals that you set for yourself or your business to achieve in terms of finances. They are important markers of progress that help you measure your financial success.

Examples of financial milestones include paying off debt, building an emergency fund, saving for retirement, buying a home, and achieving a certain net worth.

Financial milestones can vary depending on your personal or business financial goals, but they should be specific, measurable, and realistic.

TYPES OF FINANCIAL MILESTONES
Short-Term Milestones

Short-term financial milestones are goals that can be achieved within one to two years. These may include establishing an emergency fund, paying off a credit card, or saving for a vacation.

Medium-Term Milestones

Medium-term financial milestones typically take two to five years to achieve. Examples include saving for a down payment on a home, paying off student loans, or starting a small business. These milestones require more planning and perseverance but are essential for long-term financial stability.

Long-Term Milestones:

Long-term financial milestones can take five years or more to achieve. These may include funding retirement accounts, saving for children's education, or achieving financial independence.

Long-term milestones require consistent effort and a long-term vision but ultimately lead to financial security and freedom.

COMMON FINANCIAL MILESTONES
Establishing an Emergency Fund

An emergency fund is a savings account designed to cover unexpected expenses, such as job loss, medical emergencies, or urgent home repairs. Financial experts recommend having three to six months' worth of living expenses saved in an emergency fund.

- Paying Off High-Interest Debt:

High-interest debt, such as credit card balances, can be detrimental to financial health. Paying off these debts should be prioritized to reduce interest costs and improve cash flow.

- Saving for a Down Payment on a Home:

Homeownership is a significant financial milestone for many individuals and families. Saving for a down payment requires discipline and patience but can lead to long-term financial benefits, such as building equity and tax advantages.

FINANCIAL MISTAKES TO AVOID

Here we'll take a look at some of the most common financial mistakes that often lead people to major economic hardship. Even if you're already facing financial difficulties, steering clear of these mistakes could be the key to survival.

1. Excessive and Frivolous Spending

Great fortunes are often lost one dollar at a time. It may not seem like a big deal when you pick up that double-mocha cappuccino or have dinner out or order that pay-per-view movie, but every little item adds up.

Just $25 per week spent on dining out costs you $1,300 per year, which could go toward an extra credit card or auto payment or several extra payments. If you're enduring financial hardship, avoiding this mistake really matters—

after all, if you're only a few dollars away from foreclosure or bankruptcy, every dollar will count more than ever.

2. Never-Ending Payments

Ask yourself if you really need items that keep you paying every month, year after year. Things like cable television, music services, or high-end gym memberships can force you to pay unceasingly but leave you owning nothing. When money is tight, or you just want to save more, creating a leaner lifestyle can go a long way to fattening your savings and cushioning yourself from financial hardship.

3. Living on Borrowed Money

Using credit cards to buy essentials has become somewhat commonplace. But even if an ever-increasing number of consumers are willing to pay double-digit interest rates on gasoline, groceries, and a host of other items that are gone long before the bill is paid in full, it's not wise financial advice to do so. Credit card interest rates make the price of the charged items a great deal more expensive. In some cases, using credit can also mean you'll spend more than you earn.

4. Buying a New Car

Millions of new cars are sold each year, although few buyers can afford to pay for them in cash. However, the inability to pay cash for a new car can also mean an inability to afford the car. After all, being able to afford the payment is not the same as being able to afford the car.

Furthermore, by borrowing money to buy a car, the consumer pays interest on a depreciating asset, which amplifies the difference between the value of the car and the price paid for it. Worse yet, many people trade in their cars every two or three years and lose money on every trade.

Sometimes a person has no choice but to take out a loan to buy a car, but how many consumers really need a large SUV? Such vehicles are expensive to buy, insure, and fuel. Unless you tow a boat or trailer or need an SUV to earn a living, it can be disadvantageous to purchase one.

If you need to buy a car and/or borrow money to do so, consider buying one that uses less gas and costs less to insure and maintain. Cars are expensive, and if you're buying more of a car than you need, you might be burning through money that could have been saved or used to pay off debt.

5. Spending Too Much on Your House

When it comes to buying a house, bigger is not necessarily better. Unless you have a large family, choosing a 6,000-square-foot home will only mean more expensive taxes, maintenance, and utilities. Do you really want to put such a significant, long-term dent in your monthly budget?

6. Using Home Equity like a Piggy Bank

Refinancing and taking cash out of your home means giving away ownership to someone else. In some cases, refinancing might make sense If you can lower your rate or if you can refinance and pay off higher-interest debt.

However, the other alternative is to open a home equity line of credit (HELOC). This allows you to effectively use the equity in your home like a credit card. This could mean paying unnecessary interest for the sake of using your home equity line of credit.1

7. Living Paycheck to Paycheck

In June 2021, the U.S. household personal savings rate was 9.4%.2 Many households may live paycheck to paycheck, and an unforeseen problem can easily become a disaster if you are not prepared.

The cumulative result of overspending puts people into a precarious position—one in which they need every dime they earn and one missed paycheck would be disastrous. This is not the position you want to find yourself in when an economic recession hits. If this happens, you'll have very few options.

Many financial planners will tell you to keep three months' worth of expenses in an account where you can access it quickly. Loss of employment or changes in the economy could drain your savings and place you in a cycle of debt paying for debt. A three-month buffer could be the difference between keeping or losing your house.

8. Not Investing in Retirement

If you do not get your money working for you in the markets or through other income-producing investments, you may never be able to stop working. Making monthly contributions to designated retirement accounts is essential for a comfortable retirement.

Take advantage of <u>tax-deferred retirement accounts</u> and/or your employer-sponsored plan. Understand the time your investments will have to grow and how much risk you can tolerate. Consult a qualified <u>financial advisor</u> to match this with your goals if possible.

9. Paying Off Debt with Savings

You may be thinking that if your debt is costing 19% and your retirement account is making 7%, swapping the retirement for the debt means you will be pocketing the difference. But it's not that simple.

In addition to losing the power of <u>compounding</u>, it's very hard to pay back those retirement funds, and you could be hit with hefty fees. With the right mindset, borrowing from your retirement account can be a viable option, but even the most disciplined planners have a tough time placing money aside to rebuild these accounts.

When the debt gets paid off, the urgency to pay it back usually goes away. It will be very tempting to continue spending at the same pace, which means you could go back into debt again. If you are going to pay off debt with savings, you have to live like you still have a debt to pay— to your retirement fund.

10. Not Having a Plan

Your financial future depends on what is going on right now. People spend countless hours watching TV or scrolling through their social media feeds, but setting aside two hours a week for their finances is out of the question.

You need to know where you are going. Make spending some time planning your finances a priority.

The Bottom Line

To steer yourself away from the dangers of overspending, start by monitoring the little expenses that add up quickly, then move on to monitoring the big expenses. Think carefully before adding new debts to your list of payments, and keep in mind that being able to make a payment isn't the same as being able to afford the purchase. Finally, make saving some of what you earn a monthly priority, along with spending time developing a sound financial plan.